HENRY CISNEROS

Henry Cisneros addresses the 1984 Democratic
National Convention in San Francisco.

HENRY CISNEROS
Mexican-American Mayor

By Naurice Roberts

CHILDRENS PRESS®
CHICAGO

Cover: Mayor Henry G. Cisneros

p. 3   From left to right: Helen Ayala, president of C.O.P.S.; Henry Cisneros, mayor of San Antonio; Maria Berrizobal, city council member at a planning meeting for Vista Verde South

Picture Acknowledgements:

Wide World Photos—1, 29

Journalism Services/© Oscar Williams—Cover: 2, 3, 6 (left), 14, 15, 17, 18, 19 (2 photos), 20 (3 photos), 22, 23, 24 (2 photos), 25, 26, 31, 32

Courtesy of Central Catholic Marianist High School—5, 10 (2 photos)

UPI/Bettman Newsphotos—27 (2 photos) 29, 30

San Antonio Convention & Visitors Bureau—6 (right), 7, 8 (2 photos)

Texas A & M University—13, (2 photos)

Library of Congress Cataloging-in-Publication Data

Roberts, Naurice.
    Henry Cisneros: Mexican-American Mayor.

    Summary: A biography of the young Mexican American mayor of San Antonio who was considered as a candidate for Vice-President of the United States in 1984.
    1. Cisneros, Henry—Juvenile literature.
2. Mayors—Texas—San Antonio—Biography—Juvenile literature.   3. San Antonio (Tex.)—Politics and government—Juvenile literature.   [1. Cisneros, Henry.
2. Mayors.   3. Mexican Americans]   I. Title.
II. Series.
F394.S2C567   1986   976.4'351063'0924   [B] [92]   85-29057
ISBN 0-516-03485-5

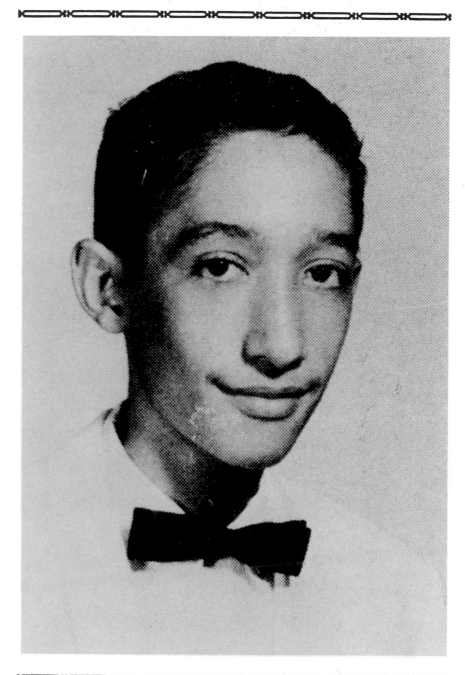

1964 class picture

Who is Henry G. Cisneros, and why is he important?

Henry Cisneros is a first. He is the first American of Mexican descent ever elected mayor of an important city—San Antonio, Texas. Many people strongly believe that Henry Cisneros is one of the youngest and smartest politicians in America today.

Henry Cisneros is the mayor of the tenth largest city in the United States. Despite modern constructions, San Antonio retains much of its old world charm.

Mariachi bands play along *Paseo del Rio*, (River Walk), during the ten days of Fiesta San Antonio.

Henry is proud of his Mexican heritage. His grandfather, Jose Romulo Munguia y Torres, crossed the Rio Grande from Mexico into the United States in 1926. He settled in San Antonio, Texas. Like other immigrants before and after him, Munguia came to the U.S. to seek a better life for his family.

He worked hard, and, in time, bought a small house on the west side of San Antonio.

In 1944, Munguia's daughter, Elvira, met George Cisneros, one of her brother's army buddies. Six months later, she and George were married. Two years later, on June 11, 1947, Henry Gabriel Cisneros was born.

Henry grew up in his grandfather's pleasant, middle-class, Hispanic neighborhood. All the neighbors were good friends. They always helped each other. Many times they would come together and share holidays and other special occasions.

For four nights during Fiesta San Antonio, the La Villita Historical District (left) becomes a cultural fair. The *Escaramuza*, a precision sidesaddle riding team (above), made up of young women from 12 to 18, is part of the fiesta's *charreada*, or Mexican rodeo.

Henry's grandfather taught the family to be proud of their heritage. Sometimes the family would get together and study Mexican culture and history. Henry and his brothers and sisters—Pauline, George, Jr., Tina, and Tim—listened and learned.

Elvira and George Cisneros believed in hard work and education. They wanted their children to be successful. Mrs. Cisneros kept the children busy and out of trouble. Everyone had something special to do—even during summer vacation.

Henry's hobbies included building model airplanes and playing the piano. Sometimes he would write stories and poems with his brothers and sisters. He also liked to read. He liked it so much that one summer he read nearly fifty books!

Henry (first seat, row two) played French horn in his high school band. A leader in the sodality, Henry (standing top right, above) was interested in his own and his classmates spiritual development.

The family would talk for hours after dinner. George Cisneros and his children discussed different issues and current events.

Henry was smart and energetic. He was so smart that he was skipped from second to fourth grade.

The future mayor was really challenged at Central Catholic High School. He studied and learned as much as he could. A teacher encouraged him to express himself by writing. When President John F. Kennedy was killed in 1963, Henry was sixteen. He wrote a poem about the tragic death of this young president. It was selected as one of the most outstanding poems in all of San Antonio's high schools and was included in a special book of poetry.

Henry did well outside the classroom, too. He played the French horn and was executive officer in the ROTC. At this time he thought about having a military career like his father, who was a colonel, but college came first. After graduation he entered Texas A & M University.

Soon, he became a class officer and was named outstanding cadet of his ROTC unit. Henry liked college. At first he had too much fun. Once a professor scolded him because some of his grades weren't good. Henry even had to repeat a course. It never happened again. Next time the young cadet received all A's! Henry became a top competitor. His new goal was to become the best and to "go for it!"

Thinking about the future, Henry decided he wanted a career in government. After graduation he began working for the cities of San Antonio and Bryan, Texas.

Later he worked for the Model Cities Program in San Antonio. This was an important government program that helped poor people. He enjoyed the work. This was a busy time for Henry. But he was not too busy to marry his high-school sweetheart, Mary Alice Perez, on June 1, 1969.

Far left: Henry (in the first row, right) served on the student leadership committee in college at Texas A & M. *Left:* The year before he had been treasurer of the sophomore class, (Cisneros is second from left).

However, Henry decided he didn't know enough about government even though he had a master's degree from Texas A & M University. So he and Mary Alice headed for Washington, D.C., where Henry enrolled at Georgetown University. He also began working at the National League of Cities.

There he learned about city problems and how to solve them. He then made a very important decision.

He decided that someday he would return home and become mayor of San Antonio. But first he had a lot of work to do. He must be prepared.

Washington, D.C., fascinated Henry. He decided to learn still more about government. So he applied for a special program called the White House Fellows. If accepted, he would work in the White House or with cabinet members. It was a great opportunity.

Mayor Cisneros conducts a bus tour of real estate sites available for development by private businesses.

Henry jogs with
his daughter
Teresa.

In 1971 Henry Cisneros became a
White House Fellow. He was one of
sixteen persons selected from a group
of three thousand! That same year
his first daughter, Teresa, was born.

His job was with Elliot
Richardson, secretary of health,
education, and welfare. Again, this
was a wonderful chance to work on
city problems.

Elliot Richardson thought Henry
was a talented and skillful young
man. He liked him and encouraged
Henry's political plans.

During Henry's last year as a White House Fellow he visited Africa and Asia. Returning to the United States, he decided to attend Harvard University in Cambridge, Massachusetts, for even more education. He later attended the Massachusetts Institute of Technology and was a teacher. Henry received another master's degree and a doctorate, the highest college degree.

In August, 1974, Henry and Mary Alice decided it was time to return home. Dr. Henry Cisneros would become an assistant professor at the University of Texas at San Antonio. The Cisneros family would eventually live in Grandfather Munguia's modest, gray frame house in the old west side neighborhood.

Mary Alice and Henry Cisneros admire a neighbor's child in their west side neighborhood.

Everything was very confusing when Henry returned home. The Mexican-Americans were struggling to gain political power. The whites who controlled city government were resisting them. Neither group trusted the other. Hispanics had the voting power—they were the largest single ethnic group in the city. Now they wanted to elect one of their own to political office.

The search was on for someone everyone could trust. People turned to Henry Cisneros. He had the government experience. A few people thought he wasn't the right person for the job. But after a while all agreed. The Hispanics backed Henry.

In 1975 Henry Cisneros became the youngest city councilman in San Antonio history. In that year his second daughter, Mercedes Christina, was born.

The Cisneros family, from left to right: Mercedes, Henry, Teresa, Mary Alice

Before becoming mayor, Henry served on the city council (right) for six years.

The new city councilman worked very hard trying to bring the people of San Antonio together. He always voted for the programs that he thought were best for the city. The people liked Henry. They liked him so much they reelected him in 1977 and again in 1979.

Devoted parents Henry and Mary Alice include
Teresa and Mercedes in their public appearances.
Wearing a T-shirt proclaiming San Antonio
"America's Town All-American 1983," Henry (above)
plays football with the neighborhood boys.

A mayoral election was to be held in 1981. Henry thought about his political plans. This was really his big chance. He decided to run for mayor of San Antonio.

Family members, childhood friends, union leaders, young people, senior citizens, political workers—everyone came together to work for Henry Cisneros.

They raised money, knocked on doors, talked on the telephone, gave speeches, and stuffed envelopes. It was a hard fight, but Henry Cisneros won! On April 4, 1981, he became the first Hispanic mayor of a major U.S. city. He took the oath of office on May 1.

Mayor Cisneros studies telephone messages in his office.

The new mayor had to work
harder than ever before. There were
still some bad feelings after the
election. So he continued working to
bring everyone together.

Henry promised to get jobs for
people and bring new high-tech
business to the city. This was part of
his economic growth program. San
Antonio, like other cities in the
United States needed this help.

In order to attract new businesses to the city, Mayor Cisneros must travel outside his state, giving speeches and attending planning meetings with potential investors.

Mayor Cisneros takes Andrew Young, mayor of Atlanta, Georgia, along River Walk.

In 1983 Henry was reelected by a very large vote. He had kept his promises. Things were improving in the city. People were getting along better, too.

By now, the entire country was talking about the young Mexican-American mayor from San Antonio. He was asked to give speeches, to talk to Congress and different groups all over the country.

Mayor Cisneros answers questions from reporters during the 1984 Democratic Convention.

Reporters and writers from newspapers, magazines, and television and radio stations all wanted interviews with him. He had become a national figure. Henry was busier than ever. Even though he was mayor, he still kept his job at the university.

The year 1984 proved to be very exciting for Mayor Cisneros. He was becoming more and more involved in national politics. Walter Mondale, who was running for president, was a friend. He asked Henry to speak at the Democratic National Convention and work with Hispanic delegates.

Henry gave a good speech. The next time Walter Mondale asked Henry to speak was at a press conference. The mayor of San Antonio was being interviewed for the job of vice-president of the United States.

After an interview, Henry and Walter Mondale, the Democratic presidential candidate, talked to the press. Later the Cisneros family posed with Mondale (above, left) and his wife Joan (above, right).

Democratic presidential candidate Mondale was looking for a vice-presidential running mate who would attract voters in each of the fifty states. He was very impressed with Henry Cisneros. So, Henry and his family went to Mondale's home in Minnesota. This was a great honor. Henry and Mondale had a private talk. He was the only Mexican-American ever considered for this position.

However, the mayor was not selected. He was the second choice. Congresswoman Geraldine Ferraro ran for vice-president with Walter Mondale. (She was the first woman ever picked to run for this office.)

Henry campaigned for Mondale and Ferraro, but they lost. Ronald Reagan was elected to serve a second term as president.

Today many political experts see

Cisneros as a shining star in the national Democratic party and a strong outstanding leader for the Hispanic community. Some say he could even go all the way to the White House one day.

In addition to being recognized politically, Henry Cisneros has also been honored by a number of groups and organizations.

He received the "Outstanding Young Man of San Antonio" award, an "Outstanding Young Texans" award, an "Outstanding Young Men

The five outstanding Texans chosen by the Texas Jaycees from left to right: Henry Cisneros, San Antonio; Michael Moore, Houston; Ralph Murillo, El Paso; Glyn Strotter, Dallas; and Mervin Peters, Bryan.

Selwa Roosevelt, Chief of Protocol, right, swears in the Central American Commission (from left); Henry G. Cisneros, Richard M. Scammon, Carlos F. Diaz-Alejandro, Wilson S. Johnson, Justice Potter Stewart, William P. Clements, Jr., Nicholas F. Brady, Robert S. Strauss, John Silber, William B. Walsh, and Henry Kissinger.

of America" award, the "Torch of Liberty" and "Tree of Life" and "Alumni Achievement" awards and many more.

The mayor has served on many committees and councils. President Ronald Reagan even asked him to serve on a special committee on Central America.

Henry Cisneros is a person everyone should know. He is a Mexican-American who, like his immigrant grandfather, believes very strongly in this country.

Proud of his roots, the young mayor of San Antonio, Texas, has accomplished much so far in his life. He is looking toward a bright future. And many Americans will be looking, too, as he continues to move forward.

HENRY CISNEROS

TIMELINE

1947	June 11—Henry Gabriel Cisneros is born in San Antonio
1961	Attended Central Catholic High School
1964	Attended Texas A & M University
1969	June 1—Married Mary Alice Perez
1970	Attended Georgetown University and worked for National League of Cities in Washington, D.C.
1971	Named White House Fellow; daughter Teresa is born
1973	Studied at Harvard University and Massachusetts Institute of Technology
1974	Returned to San Antonio and joined staff of University of Texas
1975	Elected to city council; daughter Mercedes is born
1976	Named one of the Five Outstanding Young Texans
1981	April 4—elected mayor of San Antonio
1983	Reelected mayor; appointed to serve on Central American Commission
1984	Interviewed by Walter Mondale for vice-presidential position on Democratic ticket

ABOUT THE AUTHOR

NAURICE ROBERTS has written numerous stories and poems for children. Her background includes work as a copywriter, television personality, commercial announcer, college instructor, communications consultant, and human resources trainer. She received a B.A. in Broadcast Communications from Columbia College in Chicago where she presently resides. Her hobbies include working with young people, lecturing, and jogging. She has written books about Andrew Young, Barbara Jordan, and Cesar Chavez.